Consulting

Startup Success!

Capitalize on the New Trends & Niches of Today's Consulting Business

Million Dollar Startup Solution

By

Robert R. Sullivan

Published by:

Streets of Dream
Press

Streets of Dream Press

Cover & Interior designed

By

Ron Jamieson

First Edition

What's Inside

Consulting helps companies improve their performance. It operates by analyzing current organizational problems and developing plans to resolve them. Companies use the services of consultants to gather objective, external advice, and they gain access to the specialized skills of the consultants.

A consultant becomes exposed to different problems of organizations. As such, he becomes aware of the industry's best practices. Some organizations may have difficulty adapting to some of these practices, hence the need for a consultant.

A consultant may offer help in organizational change management, and coaching skills development. He can provide services in implementing technology and process analysis. He can also help in improving operations and developing strategies. Oftentimes, he brings their own frameworks or methodologies to help him, or her identify organizational problems. He uses them to provide recommendations to his clients.

DIFFERENT CONSULTING APPROACHES

A consultant can take the prescriptive approach. He offers expert help or advice to his clients. There is less collaboration or input from the organizations. The facilitative approach requires the consultant to focus on the consultation process. It does not put weight on his technical or specific expertise.

Consulting firms sometimes follow a structured matrix. One axis is their type of consulting or business function. The other axis is the industry focus. The consultant oftentimes occupies different parts of the matrix. For instance, he can have specializations in company operations in the oil industry. Another consultant can focus on improving processes in the retail industry.

The consulting specialties are strategic management, human resource consulting, and design. They can also include engineering management, IT consulting, and virtual management consulting. Specialties can include operations management consulting, management science, etc.

Many of these specializations overlap. Large consulting firms offer diversified consultancies. Smaller firms or boutique consultancies offer specialties.

WHAT IS A CONSULTANT?

A consultant offers expert advice in areas like management, accountancy, human resources, and finance. He can provide advice in the fields of science, security, education, and law. Also, he can offer their advice on marketing, engineering, public relations and other fields. A consultant is an experienced professional in a specific area. He has an in-depth knowledge about the subject.

A consultant can be an internal consultant or an external one. An internal consultant works within the organization. He provides advice to individuals or other departments about his areas of expertise. An external consultant is not an employee of any of his clients. He works on a temporary basis in an organization for a fee. He may work for a consulting firm or be self-employed.

Through a consultant, an organization can have temporary access to expertise. It can control its expenses because it will only pay for the services as needed. Oftentimes, it receives presentations and reports from a consultant. In some instances, the organization can receive products or customized software from the consultant.

A consultant conducts his research and analysis in his office. He usually works at his client's site for some time to observe work processes and study the company's operations. He also has to interview the stakeholders in the organization.

The choice of work location depends on the interaction required with the organization's employees. Because of technology, a skilled consultant can work on online platforms as a freelancer.

QUALIFICATIONS TO BECOME A CONSULTANT

In general, there are no preset qualifications for consultants. But, most consultants have at least an undergraduate degree in their field of expertise. Some fields need professional licenses before they can practice consultancy. A legal consultant must pass the bar. An accounting consultant must pass the accounting board exam.

Some people become consultants because they have a distinguished and lengthy career in a specific field without having a higher degree in that field. Organizations may prefer consultants with government or management experience. Professional license or a college degree may not be needed.

A consultant is a person who can influence an organization, group, or individual. But, he can only recommend changes. He has no authority to instruct others to put in place his recommendations. He cannot make the decisions for his clients.

Consultants can join consulting accreditation organizations. They can do so to establish their credibility in the industry. Accredited consultants follow a Code of Ethics. They strive to provide practical advice using their experience and skills. The International Council of Management Consulting Institutes has at least 50 member institutes worldwide. It awards the Certified Management Consultant to members who pass its rigid accreditation process. National associations of consulting engineers are members of the International Federation of Consulting Engineers.

TYPES OF CONSULTING

Strategy Consulting

This is a type of consulting wherein a consultant offers high-level services. It focuses on economic policy, functional strategy, organizational and corporate strategy, and government policy. A strategy consultant focuses on developing his analytical and quantitative skills. He provides timely advice to higher management.

Management Consulting

Management consulting focuses on various concerns from strategy to other management elements. Because of this, at least half of all consultants are into management consulting.

Operations Consulting

Operations consulting helps organizations improve their operational performance. It includes activities that put in place changes in primary and secondary functions. An operations consultant often works with technology and strategy consultants.

Financial Advisory Consulting

Financial advisory consulting addresses concerns about financial and analytical capabilities of an organization. A financial advisor can practice in corporate finance, mergers and acquisitions, and tax law. He can also practice in risk management, real estate, and restructuring. Moreover, he can specialize in forensic support and research.

Human Resource Consulting

Human Resource consulting deals with problems about human capital in an organization. It also helps organizations in improving the HR department's performance. An HR consultant tackles issues on change management, organizational changes, and learning and development. He also provides advice on employment terms, retirement, and talent management.

IT Consulting

IT consulting focuses on the creation and application of IT to improve the organization. IT consultants do not perform day-to-day IT operations. Most of these IT consultants manage implementation projects.

Their responsibilities can include project management, system integration, or process management.

CHAPTER 2: CURRENT STATE OF CONSULTING BUSINESS

The 2008 - 2009 recession resulted in the growth of the consulting business. Consulting focused on advisory services, engineering consulting, management consulting, IT consulting, outsourcing, etc. In 2015, the US Census Bureau estimated the consulting industry to be worth $607 billion. Globalization helped the industry to reach new heights. Consulting firms expanded in Europe and North America, as well as in China, India, and Brazil.

Consulting firms declined when corporate budgets shrank, and the global economy slowed down. At the beginning of 2013, corporate profits began to rise. Company executives showed interest in consulting firms that can provide excellent return-on-investment. Thus, global consulting firms experienced massive growth in revenues and employee count.

Because of the economic and industry changes, consulting firms can experience significant growth.

RECESSION

Experienced and qualified professionals lost their jobs between 2008 and 2009. Instead of retiring or looking for new jobs, they worked as independent consultants. Because of this, they now dominate the consulting industry.

MERGERS AND ACQUISITIONS

Independent consultants and small consulting firms thrive because of ease of entry and low cost of operations. Also, because of mergers and acquisitions, the demand for all-inclusive consulting services grew.

EMERGING MARKETS

Up-and-coming markets, like Malaysia, Indonesia, and Russia, create more demand for consultants. Consultants who have the experience with international corporate expansion have an edge.

CHANGES IN HEALTHCARE

Companies need guidance on decreasing expenses for employee benefits. They need help in minimizing costs, increasing efficiency, and implementing digital health records.

FOCUS ON PROFITABILITY

Companies hire consultants to boost their profitability. These consultants help them in improving supply chain efficiency, cash flow, and manufacturing processes.

NEW LAWS

Companies hire consultants to assist them with new European and US laws. They need help in dealing with the healthcare, environmental, and financial government regulations.

GROWING COMPETITION AND PICKY CLIENTS

In 2009, the global consulting industry experienced a 9.1% decline. According to Kennedy Information, it was the worst year for the industry since 1982. At present, the industry is thriving because organizations began hiring consultants. Most of the consulting projects involved cutting costs in 2009. But things have changed since then. Companies now hire consultants to boost growth

Because of diversity in the industry, consultants thrive in strategy, financial, and technology consulting. Most corporations view strategy consulting as paid advisers who reinvent their businesses. Experts agree that strategy consulting may grow by as much as 1.1% annually.

Emerging markets need strategy consultants. The Big Four accounting firms buy specialist organizations in the healthcare and technology sectors. Thus, they grow in specialization, size, and geography. In the USA, these companies cannot offer consulting to their audit clients. But, they can provide a "one-stop-shop" service to other countries.

For 20 years, many consulting firms hired junior consultants. They placed them in the offices of their clients. They billed these clients by the hour. But, these clients are now refusing to pay for these junior consultants. They demand better consultants to work with their own personnel.

This means that the consulting industry is becoming a provider of temporary labor. Clients also hire smaller consulting firms, instead of the big ones. Some of them employ only a consultant as a project manager then select their employees to be part of the team. They demand value for money. Consultants now find the market competitive.

CHAPTER 3: OPPORTUNITIES IN CONSULTING

A management consultant advises organizations about particular areas that need improvement. He provides advice in the areas of talent, information technology, and logistics. He can also offer his services in marketing, strategy, and organizational design. His recommendation can include models, platforms, and processes. It can align organizations with their opportunities, challenges, external and internal threats, and strengths.

In the US, there were some 788,038 management consultants as of 2014. The number can increase by as much as 19% by 2022. Most of these consultants see their career as temporary, as they want to have a full-time career in a company. The majority of them see themselves as consultants for up to five years then move into full-time with the company they are consulting. Money doesn't seem to be a factor because many of these consultants earn around $141,000.

In 2015, Global Industry Analysts, Inc. estimated the global IT consulting market to be $255 billion. Some of the drivers of growth included strong demand and a shortage of talent. The increased role of consulting in globalization and offshoring were drivers of growth. The superiority of foreign labor also helped the industry grow.

Organizations hire an IT consultant to help them meet their needs. As such, an experienced and expert IT consultant on disruptive technologies is more valuable. On the average, he earns around $72,000 per annum, depending on where he lives and his experience. If he has his own IT consulting firm, he can earn more money.

A consultant can also practice in other niches like education, environmental, and financial services. He can offer his consulting services on human resources, engineering, and marketing. Each of these niches has its own outlook, salary, and skill sets, along with its opportunities and challenges.

INCREASED SEGMENTATION AND SPECIALIZATION

The 2015 Management Consulting Benchmark Report showed that industry expertise is important for consultants. Consulting firms have an advantage if they pursue projects based on function and size. Large companies focus on strategy-oriented engagements on a global scale. Smaller and specialized consulting firms concentrate on operations, organization transformation, strategy, and risk management. Some consulting firms are now targeting non-profit organizations, quasi-government agencies, and government agencies. Other consulting firms offer retail sales analysis and IT deployment.

CONSULTING IN THE ENERGY SECTOR

Consultants bring their experience and expertise to the energy sector. Energy companies need consulting services for smart grids, which use automation and technology. They need to make their operations energy efficient. Consulting involves smart distribution, smart metering, and supply chain management in smart electricity.

DEVELOPING ALLIANCES AND PARTNERSHIPS

Consulting firms build strategic relationships so that they can use their collaborative strengths. Accenture and Siemens have a joint venture to provide consulting services for sustainable energy. Accenture has the knowledge and resources while Siemens has the energy expertise.

WORKING IN VIRTUAL TEAMS

Today, consulting firms now work with virtual projects and teams. One of the challenges with virtual teams is the failure to read and understand nonverbal cues. Consultants do not have time to build relationships during virtual meetings. Virtual team members lack collegiality, trust, and rapport. It is challenging to manage conflict and make sound decisions. Virtual team members find it challenging to express their options.

Consulting firms that prefer virtual teams must overcome such challenges to be successful. Most of these firms want to go virtual because it offers more freedom to consultants. Also, virtual teams offer money savings over the long term.

BUDGET CUTS IN GOVERNMENTS

Due to low tax revenues, European and US governments experience budget cuts. As such, consulting firms that provide services to them face new challenges. They must deliver excellent results like reduce debt, or increase revenue. They must make improvements by implementing strategic initiatives. Governments now focus on return-on-investment.

CHAPTER 4: FINDING AND MASTERING A NICHE

If you want to be a consultant, you need to have a niche. A niche is a segment of the market that you can focus to serve. People in that particular niche have needs that you can help meet. For instance, a niche on pets and pet products can be ferret foot care, but this niche may not be big enough for you to earn a living.

Consulting is a broad market. Project management is a niche but is also big. Many consultants offer project management services. They have the project management skills, experience, and credentials. You may find it difficult to penetrate this niche. Thus, you may charge a lower rate to get clients. If you want to be a consultant, you need to find a niche with less competition, yet big enough for you to earn a living.

Career advisors may tell you to focus on a smaller niche. You need to specialize so that your consulting business can thrive. You will encounter less competition in a specialized niche. Also, you can charge more money per hour because of your specialized skills.

5 REASONS FOR TARGETING A NICHE

Less Competition

If you have experience or specialized skills in a niche, you can get more clients. Not all consultants have your expertise.

Earn More Money

Because you have more specialized skills, you can charge more per hour for your services.

More Clients

If you are providing consulting services to a niche, potential clients will seek you out. They need someone with knowledge and skills to serve their needs better.

Entry Barriers

Not all consultants can provide their services to a particular niche. If you have the necessary skills set for it, you will not have many competitors. Thus, you can charge higher rates. For example, not everyone can put in place a particular automation project. If you have the skills set for it, you can offer your services to that particular niche.

Less Marketing Effort

If there is less competition, you need not exert a lot of effort to market your consulting services. You become popular as an expert. As such, potential customers come to you.

6 WAYS TO FINDING A CONSULTING NICHE

Check Your Skills and Experience

If you want to be a consultant, you must first assess your skills and experience. You must use your talents to market to your prospective clients.

Decide on Your Best Marketable Skills

After listing down your skills and experience, decide which of these skills you do best. You need to determine which of them you like most.

Find Out Demand for Your Skills

Once you know your marketable skills, check if there is a high demand for them.

Determine How Much Clients Pay for Your Skills

Discover what the average pay a consultant receives for your most marketable skills.

Narrow Down Skills Set

Decide on your specialty. If you are good in project management, you can focus on SalesForce implementation. If you have skills in web development, you can decide to focus on e-commerce. In essence, you need to narrow down your skills set and decide on offering it to lucrative niches.

Performing Market Research

If you want to learn about your target market, you can use keyword research. You can know the number of people searching for a specific phrase or word online through it. Through the search volume statistics, you will know the competitor websites for a keyword. You will also learn how much money these websites are paying for Google ads. Through keyword research, you can gather information about your target market.

The strategy is to find high volume keywords with low competition. You can use Market Samurai or Google AdWords. You save time with Market Samurai because it has reporting and automation features, however, you need to pay a one-time subscription for it.

How to Search for Profitable Niches

Know Who Your Competitors Are

Search for your potential competitors online. Learn about the other consultants who are serving your niche. If you cannot find a competitor in your chosen niche, you may not earn good money from it.

Check Salary Surveys

You will know if your niche is profitable if you check how much money the other consultants are charging. For example, you have two possible niches. Niche B pays a higher salary. Thus, you need to concentrate on providing your services to it.

Salary is often private. You can try calling your potential competitors to ask them about their fees, or try calling other consulting firms to learn about their rate structure. You can also get information online. You need to use keywords often used in your niche to know about reported salary ranges.

Find Out about Advertising Expense

If you need to spend a lot of money on marketing in a particular niche, you need to charge more to recoup the costs. This means that the niche is profitable if consultants pay more money to advertise. As such, you can compare advertising costs across different niches to assess profitability.

For example, Niche A charges higher advertising costs. Thus, it may be more profitable because consultants are willing to pay more for it. You can use Google AdWords to learn about advertising costs. You need to check how many advertisers are willing to pay per click for a particular keyword.

Money and Time Savings for the Client

If you can offer money and time savings to your clients, you will become a successful consultant, but have a definite amount that you can offer to them. If you can offer more time and money savings, you are in a profitable niche.

Profitability of the Client's Business

If your potential clients make a lot of money, you can charge them a higher rate. Your clients must be able and willing to pay for your services. You need to provide value for their money. Usually, clients do not mind paying more if they can get their money's worth.

Creating Re-sellable Goods and Services

You can earn more money if you can offer goods or services that you can resell to your potential clients. This will ensure that your clients become your repeat customers. You can also create a product or service that you can offer to different clients. For example, you can offer an e-course that you can teach to different clients anytime.

10 MOST PROFITABLE AND EASY NICHES FOR CONSULTANTS

Gardening Consultant

People are now investing in their houses. They spend more time at home. The home improvement industry is an expanding market. Gardening and outdoor landscaping are becoming popular. Homeowners hire gardening consultants to help them with their outdoor living spaces. You can also specialize in traditional English, cottage-style, or water gardens.

Green Living Consultant

Everyone is into environmental protection and green living. Individuals and corporations are becoming aware that they need to be good to the world they live in. Some governments even offer corporations some economic incentives for implementing environment-friendly strategies. Homeowners pay lower utility and water bills if they make their houses energy efficient. If you are knowledgeable about green living, you can provide consulting services. You can have homeowners and business owners as clients.

Home Office Design Consultant

Freelancers and business owners who run their business from home need a functional home office. Working from home is becoming popular. As such, there is a great demand for home office design consultants. If you are an expert designer, you can help clients by creating an efficient and secure space for them. You can also specialize in a telecommuting consultancy. You may offer to set up telecommuting programs for governments.

Organization and Efficiency Consultant

If you are an organization and efficiency expert, you can serve over-extended families. Small business owners and busy professionals can take advantage of your services. You can help them organizes their rooms so that they can gain effective control of their work and home life.

Color Consultant

If you are an interior designer, you can help organizations choose the best colors for areas or rooms. As a color consultant, you can help hospitals choose colors for cancer treatment centers. You can also help retail stores choose colors to stimulate the customers' buying behaviors.

Millennial Marketing Consultant

Small and medium-sized enterprises are now attracting young professionals. Baby boomers are retiring. Cities compete with each other to attract young workers. They offer career options, cultural opportunities, diversity, and entertainment venues. Smaller communities hire millennial consultants to help them tap their future workforce.

Corporations seek the help of millennial consultants to understand this particular demographic. They need help in marketing to millennial consumers. Millennial consultants help organizations to resolve the communication gap between workers.

Second Career Consultant

Individuals, such as the working retired, serial entrepreneurs, and baby boomers seek a second career. They hire consultants to help them find another successful career. These individuals need advice on pursuing a different job.

Business Transition Consultant

Consultants help companies that are transitioning from one phase to another. Small and medium-sized enterprises need help in preparing for the next growth level. Some companies are on the verge of undergoing mergers or acquisitions. Businesses searching for fresh market opportunities can also be a target market.

Image and Style Consultant

At present, individuals seek help to develop their personal grooming and fashion style. They are career men and women, trendsetting teenagers, and community volunteers. They can also be new moms who need to adapt to their new lifestyles and bodies. Professional fundraisers can also be a target market.

Home Security Consultant

Homeowners seek advice on their computer systems' security vulnerabilities. They also hire security consultants to help them with their physical security issues. These people want to protect their homes from invasions. Network security specialists help homeowners protect their computers against malware, spyware, and viruses.

CHAPTER 5: MASTERING A NICHE

Once you found a niche, a subject you are comfortable in and believe you can master the niche enough to be able to consult people, it is time to master that niche. It is time to become a pro at that niche. But to get there, you must spend long hours on improving your skills.

You can take advantage of numerous online resources like articles, audio interviews, instructional videos, and other training materials. You can also search for institutions that offer certifications in your chosen field. Often, you can learn about best practices, fundamentals, and insights about your niche. Some institutions offer online programs for certifications.

BENEFITS OF CONSULTING CERTIFICATIONS

Nowadays, there are plenty of online interactive courses you can find that can teach you almost anything. If you can sign up for one these courses, you can learn and develop practical approaches and skills that you can use in your business. You spend hours learning from video modules, books, and expert audio interviews.

You become competent in consultancy by learning from the mistakes of experts. You can grow your practice through service execution and superior positioning. If you are a certified consultant, you generate more consulting opportunities.

WHO CAN PARTICIPATE IN A CONSULTING CERTIFICATION

(1) A person who wants to master the consulting fundamentals, best practices, and trade secrets.

(2) A working person who wants to become a consultant in the future.

(3) A consultant who wants to master his profession.

(4) A consultant who wants to develop thought leadership and world-class educational components to establish dominance in his chosen niche.

(5) A consultant who wants to learn new concepts to use in his area of expertise.

HOW TO BE THE BEST CONSULTANT

Do What You Said You Will Do

It is important that you fulfill your promise on time. You can build credibility and trust not only with your clients but with your team as well. Your team will rely on your support for their tasks. You must keep your promises, master the basic skills, and become consistent in the quality of work that you produce. You will gain more consulting services if you can build more trust early on in your career.

Be Detail Oriented

One important skill that you must develop is to produce quality deliverables. You build trust with your clients if you can provide thorough and solid recommendations. Your documents must be free of spelling and grammatical mistakes and errors. If the recommendations contain calculations, the numbers must be correct. The quality of your work reflects on your abilities as a consultant.

Develop a Specialized Skill

If you are just starting your consultancy business, you may float between areas, industries, and clients. But, you must start to develop a skill that will keep you ahead of your competitors. You must spend the time to search for skills that you can develop.

Think Before You Act

Your ambition can be your stepping stone to be an excellent consultant. But, to become the best, you must learn critical thinking. For instance, your client wants to identify the areas where he can save money in the supply chain. But, you must first understand his business. You must assess how much money he is losing, as well as how the competitors' product prices are affecting your client's business. You need to spend time thinking through the process before you interpret the numbers.

Be Resourceful

As you go about being a consultant, you may face problems that are new to you. You need to rely on your resourcefulness to succeed. Using your creativity, you must develop your ability to solve these problems as soon as possible. In general, faced with adversity, you must seek the help of your team, your peers and internal aspects, and other external resources. Other people can help you solve these new problems.

Ask Good Questions

You must ask right questions to help you understand what you need to do. You need to learn about your client's issues. You must ask for clarifications in a non-annoying and helpful way. You can structure your questions before you approach your client.

HOW TO USE LINKEDIN

A LinkedIn account can help you win new consulting contracts and strengthen your current business. If you maintain a LinkedIn account, possible clients can find you if your profile matches the keywords they use. Your account can show up in their search results if you use the right keywords in your profile.

You can also search for new prospects in the networks of colleagues or former clients. You can reach out to these potential customers through your trusted contacts. Word-of-mouth referrals are important. Your LinkedIn connections can refer you to their contacts. Thus, you must ensure that you have a strong relationship with them. You also help them reach out to people you know.

If you have a LinkedIn account, you can take a proactive approach by reaching out to new clients through referrals from former colleagues and past clients. You can even find qualified subcontractors and staff if your business grows. Your past clients and colleagues can endorse you while you are establishing your reputation.

Also, you can prove your expertise in the consulting field by providing answers and solutions through LinkedIn Answers. You can help other professionals while solidifying your expertise.

What You Can Do with LinkedIn

(1) Establish connections with your former and existing clients. Their referrals can help you get consulting contracts. Also, you can search their networks for new clients.

(2) Reconnect with former coworkers and colleagues. These people can also refer you to their networks.

(3) Connect with people who have referred or recommended you. You can maximize your network if you connect with people who trust you.

(4) Request recommendations from former colleagues or previous clients. Potential clients will choose you if other people recommend you.

HOW TO OPTIMIZE YOUR LINKEDIN PROFILE

Create an eye-catching and effective headline

The headline, which is below your LinkedIn name, is visible in other people's home feed, group discussions, and search results. You need to edit it to include a short description of services and keywords. But, the headline has a 120-character limit.

Tell Your Story in the Summary

You must write your professional qualifications, history, and goals in the Summary section. Potential clients must be curious and interested in your values, passions, and accomplishments. Also, you must include a call to action by directing them to your personal website or email address.

Include Details in the Experience Section

You include your past work experience in this section. Instead of listing all your past projects, you can list your experience by category or by the client. Also, you can add photos, videos, documents, links, and presentations.

Show Your Credibility and Professionalism in the Skills and Endorsements Section

In the Skills section, you list your experience pertinent to the industry you are serving. You can also include testimonials and endorsements. You can ask your former clients to write a recommendation in this section.

Build Your Connections

You must maintain a visible and active LinkedIn presence by connecting with your colleagues, industry leaders, and past and present clients. You can share business updates and relevant news.

Also, you can link your website or blog to your LinkedIn account. You can join groups to build your own voice in the industry.

CHAPTER 6: SETTING UP YOUR CONSULTING BUSINESS

LICENSES AND PERMITS

Governments collect taxes from the revenues of citizens. Moreover, permits and licenses also protect the public. For example, aviation, agriculture, and alcohol are regulated in the USA. Businesses in these industries need to apply for specific permits and licenses.

Also, governments need professional licenses for doctors, veterinarians, and dentists. Business owners who sell products and services have to get a sales tax permit. Sole proprietors and home-based businesses also need to apply for a permit to operate.

Depending on the location and industry, you may need licenses and permits to be a consultant. If you are a consultant in the US, you need to get a federal tax identification number and register with state and local governments for their local taxes.

Even if your consultancy is a home-based business, you will need permits to operate it. You can check with your local or state government for requirements. In the US, you need to get a Home Occupation Permit. You also need to check with your homeowner's association. The organization may have restrictions on business activities in your community.

If you get your business permits, you must be aware of the renewal dates. Ensure that your licensing documents are in a safe and secure place. Most local governments mandate that you display your licenses or permits. Also, if you are expanding your business, you may need to secure more business permits.

THE NEED FOR A BUSINESS LICENSE

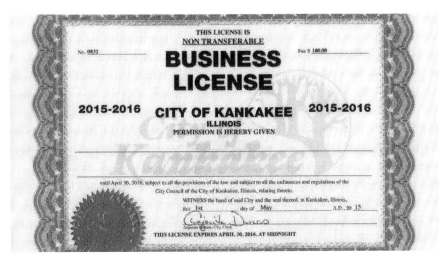

(Credit – businesslicensesolutions.com)

As a consultant, you can only accept business with clients if you have a business license. If you are going to practice in larger cities, you may need to secure more permits. Some states may need you to remit sales tax on your consulting fees. Thus, you must register your business with the department of state. Some states or counties may ask for a business name before you can conduct consultancy.

Many independent consultants do not get business licenses. They believe that they can operate their consulting business from their clients' locations. They fail to realize that they violate government guidelines when they do so. Thus, if you are a consultant, you must get a business license to avoid problems. Accusations may arise that your clients are not following labor laws if you do not have permits.

If you register your business, you qualify for business bank accounts and credit. Most clients will ask you for your Tax Identification Number for year-end reports. Legitimate clients may not get your services if you do not have a business permit.

If you are forming a specialized consulting firm, you may need more permits. You may not work on government projects without more licenses. Engineering and healthcare consulting also need industry certifications before you get a business permit.

STEPS IN FORMING A LIMITED LIABILITY COMPANY FOR A CONSULTING BUSINESS

Register the Company with the State Government

You can contact the business registration bureau where you want to provide consultancy services. You must file the necessary documents with that bureau.

Get an Employer Identification Number

In the USA, you can go to the Internal Revenue Service to get the Employer Identification Number. You may send the completed Form SS-4 through fax or email. You can fill out an online application on the IRS website.

I attached a sample IRS form SS-4 at the end of this.

Secure the Local Permits

Check with your local government for the necessary licenses you need to get to set up your business. Some consulting businesses need special licenses. You need to secure a state surety bond or private security license if you are a security consultant.

Get a D-U-N-S Number

In the USA, you need to request from Dun & Bradstreet your D-U-N-S number. Although it is voluntary, you need to get this number. Most large corporations and the federal government will not hire you if you do not have one.

ACCOUNTING CHECKLIST FOR CONSULTANTS

Decide on Your Consultancy Business Structure

You can operate as a corporation, LLC, or sole proprietor. Your business structure will determine the taxes you need to pay and the manner by which you will pay them.

Get a Tax Identification Number

In the USA, you need not use a Tax ID number if your consultancy business is a single member LLC or sole proprietor. You use your SS number instead. But, if you register as a corporation or will hire employees, you need to get a federal TIN. In other countries, you can check with your the local government about their rules on Tax ID Number.

Get a State Tax Identification Number

In the USA, some states need you to get a state tax ID number.

Decide on Your Accounting Procedures

The easiest and most convenient way to keep accounting records is to use software.

Open a Business Bank Account

Even if you operate your business as a sole proprietor, you must keep business finances in order. Thus, you need to open a bank account for it.

Get Insurance

Check with your local government about its business insurance requirements. You may want to use a professional liability insurance.

Get Certificates, Permits, and Licenses

Depending on where you want to put up your consulting business, you may need to get licenses and permits. You need to contact your local government unit about forms you need to fill up.

Choose Your Business Partners

You will need an accountant, an insurance agent, an attorney, and a banker to set up your business. These people can also serve as your business advisors as your business grows.

SETTING UP YOUR HOME OFFICE

List Important Home Office Requirements

Create a detailed list of the most important things you need for your home office. This list must include a telephone, computer, fax machine, desk, etc. You need extra space for file cabinets and a receiving room for your clients.

Pick Your Home Office Area

After listing down your home office requisites, you now have an idea how much space you need. You have to remember that this office space must be quiet and private. For example, you can dedicate a spare room for your home office. This room must have a door to filter noise from the outside. If you accept clients in your home office, you must ensure that this room is nearer the front door.

Balance Storage and Workspace Needs

Even if you have a home office, you must ensure that it is a professional one. As such, you need to plan the layout in such as way that you have ample room for work and storage. You have to remember that files and supplies must be within your reach.

Maintain Proper Lighting

You must ensure that your home office gets enough natural light. This will make your working space bright. If your office does not have ample natural lighting, you must have overhead lights. You can add desk lamps, task lighting, or floor lamps if you need lighting in a specific workspace. Also, your computer screen must not produce a glare to reduce eye strain.

Use a Business Phone

Even if you are keeping costs low, you must have a dedicated phone for your consultancy business. You must be professional in dealing with clients. Thus, your business may need a separate phone.

Get the Right Office Equipment

Aside from a dedicated phone, you must ensure that you do not skimp on important office equipment. You must invest in a sturdy desk and comfortable chair. Your computer must have efficient performance and memory. Your Internet connection must be fast.

Separate Personal and Professional Finances

You must not mix your business expenses with your personal ones. You have to ensure that you keep your business checks, records, and mails in your home office. This will make it easier for you to scrutinize business records during tax season.

Use Formal Procedures and Processes

Although there is no need to have formal rules, you must maintain efficient operations. This means that you have to standardize recordkeeping and invoice payments. You must have a process to log mileage for business trips and log time with customers. Your office ensures that information is always available if you have formal operational procedures.

Keep Office Hours

Although you can maintain flexible working hours, you may want to follow a work schedule. By making your work hours standard, you make it easier for your clients to reach you. You may work at night, but you have to ensure that your clients can reach you during traditional working hours. Moreover, you reduce distractions if you set office hours. Friends and family will not make unannounced visits or calls.

Have a Clock in Your Home Office

You should have a wall or desk clock. This way, you do not forget about the time.

CHAPTER 7: CREATING THE PRESENTATION

PowerPoint is a useful tool for you to prepare presentations for your clients. Your formal presentations, final reports, and detailed analysis can all be in PowerPoint format.

THE PYRAMID PRINCIPLE

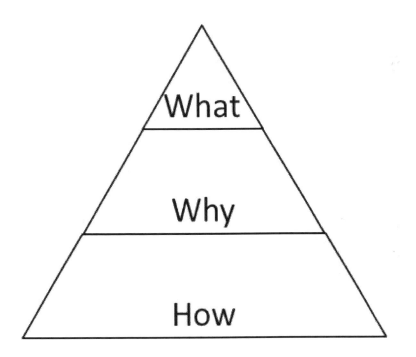

A structure is important when preparing your presentation. Your clients are busy people. Thus, your presentations must be concise and crisp. Not planning for the structure will leave your clients confused.

Consulting firms use the Pyramid Principle as a guide to the structured presentation. In essence, you need to present the information using a summary first then go into details. This means that you start with the recommendation, then proceed with supporting facts and arguments.

The Pyramid Principle will give you an opportunity to state your points. You do this before you start asking questions. It helps you focus on the essential details throughout your presentation. It is easier to create a presentation if you already have a structure.

Types of Taglines

IMPERATIVE: commands action starts with a verb
YOU TUBE – Broadcast yourself

DESCRIPTIVE: describes the product, brand or service
TED – Ideas worth spreading

SUPERLATIVE: positions the company as best in class
BUDWEISER – King of Beers

PROVOCATIVE: makes you think; typically a question
DAIRY COUNCIL – Got milk?

SPECIFIC: reveals the business category
VW – Das Auto

Taglines are critical one-sentence summaries on each slide. They help you communicate to your audience. They ensure that the readers understand the content of every slide. They are explanations your readers can learn from your presentation.

THE APPENDIX SLIDES

Your uncluttered and straightforward slides must allow your readers to follow your thoughts. Overloading the main presentation with supporting information will just overwhelm your readers. You will fail to help them understand your message if you provide tons of information on each slide.

Appendix:

- Slide 1: Cover page
- Slide 2: Executive Summary
- Slide 3:Objectives
- Slide 4: Mission Statement
- Slide 5: Company Summary
- Slides 6 & 7: Start Up Requirements
- Slide 8,9,10 & 11: Products
- Slide 12: Market Analysis Summary
- Slide 13, 14, & 15: Competition & Buying Pattern
- Slide 16: Strategy and Implementation
- Slide 17: Competitive Edge

Appendix slides are helpful if you have supporting information. They may contain testimonials and extra charts. They can also include data, process maps, and information that support your main message. You flip to these slides if questions arise.

GRAPHICS

A presentation must have simple, effective, and clear graphics. It should persuade and convince your audience. You do not have to include animations and fancy graphics to entertain and impress them. Charts should be in black and white. Three-dimensional graphics are unnecessary and can deceive your readers. Also, strive to include just one message in each chart.

DELIVERY OF PRESENTATION

You must be able to deliver your presentation in just 30 seconds. This may be difficult to do, and it takes practice, so hone your skills in such a way that you focus on your key message only.

First, define the storyline. Think about your audience and how you want to present to them. You need to decide on your background story. Your presentation must convey the message you want.

Second, define the presentation structure. Decide on how you will organize your presentation. You can do this if you understand your audience. You can use any of the three approaches: chronological, geographic, or prioritization.

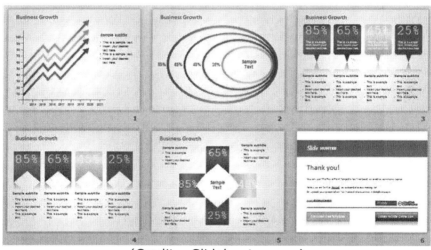

(Credit – Slidehunter.com)

The chronological approach is suitable for large projects, which have separate deliverable phases. But, it can be boring, rigorous, and long. The geographic approach is useful if your presentation compares different activities across geographies. It is a functional review of the enterprise or company. The prioritization approach is a short and direct presentation. It generates a response from the readers. You can use the pyramid principle discussed in the other section of this chapter.

Third, draft the content. You must choose only the important information in each slide. Any obvious information or marketing talk can go to the appendix slides.

Fourth, refine the content. In this step, you combine, reinvent, or throw away your slides. Your presentation must be accurate, logical, and orderly. Also, it must be professional, brief, and persuasive. By refining your presentation, you are also developing a stronger point of view.

If you have a business partner, you can collaborate with him. You can review the presentation with him so that your target audience can understand it. Remember that your clients have high expectations.

You have to ensure that you give them an excellent presentation. Collaboration can only be successful if there is mutual trust and understanding.

CHAPTER 8: PREPARING PROPOSAL TEMPLATES

SEND THE PROPOSAL AFTER REACHING AGREEMENT

You do not send a proposal to win business. You and your client must have agreed on a consultancy business before you send the proposal. Also, do not just copy a proposal online. This kind of proposal is often not effective.

Before sending the proposal, a sales conversation must take place first. Your client has to agree to offer you a contract for your consulting service. They typically should give you the go-ahead signal to send the proposal to them.

Many consultants send their proposals even if their clients are hesitant to hire them. They wonder why they do not have consulting contracts. This is because they and their clients have not yet reached an agreement.

There are a few online business service sites that can help you set up your initial proposal templates. Take a look.

https://www.proposify.com/proposal-templates/consulting-proposal-template

https://www.template.net/business/proposal-templates/consulting-proposal-template/

https://www.pandadoc.com/consulting-proposal-templates/

FOCUS ON THE CLIENT

You do not tell your client about your consulting business in the proposal. You should have discussed this with him before sending the proposal. You must use it as an opportunity and challenge to tell your client that you understand his business. Your client must have a clear understanding of the reason for hiring you as his consultant.

Focus on the Agreement

A confusing proposal will get nowhere. The prospective client will not sign it if the terms are unclear. As such, it is best that you use the proposal to confirm your agreement with your client. You must have discussed the terms of the engagement during the sales conversation.

I am attaching a sample agreement at the end of this book so you can get an idea and even take notes from it to make one for yourself.

Make the Structure of the Proposal Logical

The proposal structure must support the decision-making process. It includes the summary, goals, and project details. It discusses the responsibilities, costs, and terms of the consulting contract.

Make It Short

A proposal consists of up to 3 pages. If your proposal exceeds three pages, you have to review it. You may be including unnecessary information.

FOCUS ON THE RETURN-ON-INVESTMENT

Give a reason for your prospective client to act on your proposal. You need to convince him that his investment will reap a significant return on his business.

FOCUS ON THE OUTPUT

You need not tell your prospective client what you intend to do for him exactly, but make it clear what your client will receive when he hires your services.

USE CLEAR AND SIMPLE LANGUAGE

Do not confuse your client with legalese and jargon. Your client will not read your proposal if he does not understand it. He will let his lawyer read it before he affixes his signature. You want your proposal signed by the client as soon as possible. As such, you need to use clear and simple language.

HOW TO WRITE A PROPOSAL LETTER

Study the Project

Before you write the proposal letter, have the sales discussion with the client. Whatever you discussed in that meeting will be the basis of your proposal. Ensure that you have the necessary information before writing it.

The first paragraph of the proposal must include a discussion about the project. It must include the services you are offering and the client's goals.

Include Timelines, Duties, and Milestones

You must include your and your client's work and duties in the consulting agreement. Include details about specific milestones, and factors that may delay the completion of the project. You must also include the fees you will charge to the client.

CHAPTER 9: DESIGNING THE PRICE STRUCTURE

CONSULTING FEE MODELS

Double or Triple the Hourly Wage

To set your consulting fee, you can use your hourly wage when you were still an employee. Then, you can either double or triple it. Many consultants triple their hourly wage because of the rule of thirds. One-third of the fee goes to administration expense. The other one-third goes to other expenses, and the last one-third is their real wage. This is popular among consultants because it is easy to compute.

For example, you earn $60,000 per year plus $15,000 benefits when you were still an employee. You also receive four weeks of paid vacation. If you work 40 hours per week, you work 1920 hours a year. As such, your hourly wage is $39.06 ($75k/1920).

If you decide to double your hourly wage, you can charge $80 per hour. But, if you decide to triple your hourly wage, you need to charge $120 per hour. It is preferable to round up your consulting fee to the nearest $5 or $10. There are consultants who charge by the day, half-day, project, or other arrangements.

Daily Rate

You can also charge per Diem of consulting. To compute your daily rate, you just multiply the hourly rate by the number of working hours in a day. For example, your hourly rate is $120. You can charge $960 per day ($120 * 8 hours) or $640 per day ($80 * 8 hours).

Project-Based Rate

You can also charge per project. If you use this strategy, you need to find out the estimated number of hours you need to spend on the project. Then, you multiply this number of hours by your hourly rate. Some consultants base their rate on the benefit the client generates from their recommendations. If you know the value of your advice, you can use this in setting your consulting fee.

Performance-based Rate

Consultants can get commissions or profit shares. But, this strategy is risky. For example, if the performance of the company declines because of other factors, you may receive less than what you deserve. Also, it may take months before the client can see the results of your recommendations. In essence, you are actually giving your client an interest-free loan.

The company may be reluctant to put in place all your recommendations. Thus, you are not able to produce the full results, or you may not be able to know if the company manipulated the results to shortchange you.

You may lose your objectivity if you get a share of the profits and sharing the risk your client must assume.

Actual Data Rate

This strategy is cumbersome because it has several steps. First, you need to determine the number of working days in a year, which is 52 weeks. But, you allow six weeks for sick days, holidays, and vacation. So, you have 46 weeks or 1840 working hours per year.

Then, you need to determine your billable hours. For example, you set 50% of your time on administrative, marketing, and other tasks. Thus, you only spend 920 hours working for clients. Next, you need to consider the percentage of clients who delay their payments or never pay you. If the collection rate is 95%, you can only receive payments for 874 hours.

The next step is for you to determine how much salary you will receive if you work in a company. In our previous example, this salary may be $75,000. Your hourly consulting fee is $85.81 ($75k/874 hours). But, you need to consider overhead expenses. For example, your overhead expense is $5,000.

Divide this by 874 hours, and you get $5.72 overhead.

Then, you need to add $5.72 to $85.81. Your consulting fee per hour is $91.53. You also need to consider profit margin because you are running a business. Usually, consultants establish a profit margin between 10% and 33%. If you choose a 25% markup, your consulting fee will be $115 per hour.

Same Consulting Fee as the Others

You may consider setting your consulting fee to be the same as your competitors. Your clients may see you as someone qualified and fair.

Solution-based Rate

Over the long term, you can use a consulting fee model that represents your value as a consultant.

CHAPTER 10: HOW TO NEGOTIATE A CONSULTING CONTRACT

FOUR THINGS TO NEGOTIATE ASIDE FROM CONSULTING FEE

Travel Budget

You can negotiate with your client to shoulder your travel expenses and charge him a certain amount for your travel budget. You can make your arrangements once he pays your travel budget. You can pocket some of your travel money if you find cheap deals when you book your travels.

Content Rights

Some clients may want to own your content. They can repackage it and sell it as their own. They may also use it to train their employees. You can negotiate with your clients to keep the rights to your content. You can make more money if you use it to train employees of other companies.

High-End Coaching

After submitting your recommendations, the department heads and/or employees may need some hand-holding and training. Thus, you can negotiate high-end coaching so that you can earn more money.

Products and Services Licensing

You can earn passive income if you offer online products or courses for your customers. You can even offer these products and services as follow-up training. You can charge your client a certain amount per employee you train.

NEGOTIATING STRATEGIES

Know Your Position Before You Meet Your Client

Before you meet your client, know what you want. You can only do this if you prepare by asking the necessary questions to your prospective client. You can be successful in closing the deal if your client is comfortable in meeting you.

Understand the Expertise and Skills that Your Client Needs

Have a full understanding of the problems of your prospective client. You should know which of your experiences and skills are applicable to his requirements. You must be able to convince him that you can use your unique skills in solving his problems.

Offer a Realistic Position

Your position must be realistic to convince your client. If you are charging a higher fee, be able to provide a logical proof of your expertise.

Learn to Compromise

Exhaust all possibilities when you negotiate with your client. These possibilities will help you in closing the deal. They will promote the shared interests of your client. You can be firm about the schedule, direction, and schedule of the project, but you must be able to recognize when you need to compromise.

Focus on the Big Picture

Realize when to make a formal negotiation. Draft a strong contract and creative brief so that you do not have to deal with issues. Discussions and feedback with the client must not create conflict.

Discuss with Your Team First

If you are discussing action steps with your client, you must withhold agreement first. You must not make commitments unless you review the terms with your team. You must ensure that you and your internal team share the same goals with your prospective client.

Avoid Cultural Nuances

A client may want improvements on each deliverable during the negotiation process. You may agree to update the deliverables and project scope to please him. In some cultures, the client's negotiating position is a usual practice. You must recognize these nuances as an opportunity to improve your work.

Do Not Rush

Ensure that you iron out any detail during negotiation. You can take your time to think about these finer points before you agree on a consulting contract. If you agree immediately, your client may think that he can push his position further.

Keep the Negotiation Honest, Respectful, and Humane

The negotiation process is not a competition. You must be able to serve the needs of your client and strengthen your working relationship with him.

Know When to Walk Away

In any negotiation, you must walk away if you have used all your available options to no avail. Know when to say NO.

Do Not Take It Personally

Take every negotiation as a learning opportunity and move forward. Even if negotiations fail, analyze these failures to improve your negotiation prowess.

Failures can Lead to Future Success

Initial negotiation may fail. But, you must not close the doors with your clients and co-workers. If you are truthful and cordial, you will gain other people's respect. If you establish and reinforce clear boundaries, you generate mutual respect. You may gain a contract in the future.

Chapter 11: Getting Ready for the Project

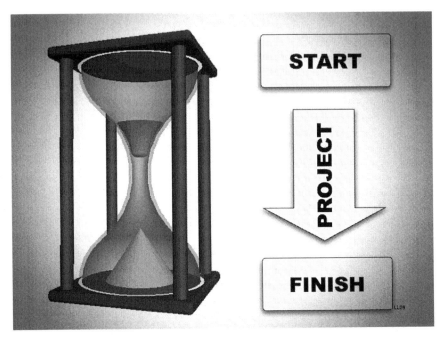

(Credit – commons.wikimedia.org)

The Welcome Kit for New Client

A welcome kit contains information you want your new clients to know. It ensures a great kick-off for your working relationship. It manages expectations before you can move forward with your consulting service. A good welcome kit enables your clients to know how you are planning to go about your consultancy with them. This way, you can correct any misinterpretations about your working relationship with them.

Give a welcome kit to all your new clients, even if the projects you have with them are small. A welcome kit is a good material that can show your professionalism and expertise. You can give it after signing the contract or send it to them in advance. Your welcome kit must be professional-looking. It must show your appreciation and respect for your new clients. It is also a representation of your consulting firm's excellence.

CONTENTS OF A WELCOME KIT

You need not include your marketing collateral in your welcome kit. You do not try to sell your services to your new client with the kit. Your welcome kit must include information about you and your consulting business. It must nurture your working relationship with your new client. It serves as a guide and reference on how you work with clients.

Your Short Biography

Your biography must include relevant and interesting facts and life experiences. It can include stories, and values about your consulting career. It must provide insights about your philosophies and belief systems about relationship and work.

Office Hours

This must include the days and times your office opens.

Communication Policies

This section includes all the possible ways your clients can reach you. It must include information about accepting phone calls and responding to emails and calls. You can also include frequency of checking voicemail and emails.

Overview of Work Processes and Operations

You can include information on the manner by which you manage your tasks and work on requests, including turnaround times.

Instructions for Work Requests Submission

You cannot accept all work requests any time. You must let your clients know that you follow protocols in dealing with their requests.

Overview of Services

You need to separate your work into categories so that you can charge per activity. For example, you offer web design and administrative support consultancies. You need to separate the tasks in administrative support and in web design. This way, you can separate the fees for each category.

Expectation

You can express your expectations to your clients. You need to let them know how they must treat you. You can tell them how they must respond to your queries, input, and feedback. Your clients should know how they can handle any misgivings. You can write your expectations in such a way that clients do not take offense from them.

Frequently-Asked-Questions

Your FAQ sheet must include a timeline of the steps that need documents completed by the client and include the other parties that will be part of the consultancy service.

You need to list the required documents from your clients. Also, you must include what the client can expect at the end of the consultancy engagement.

CHAPTER 11: COLLECTING PAYMENTS AND PAYING TAXES

(Credit —wikidot.com)

TIPS ON BILLING CLIENTS

Ask for Advance Payments

If you bill your client after each milestone, you must request him to make the payments at the start. You can also make some of the first payments higher than the rest. This way, you have a financial head start. You also reduce the risk of late payments or non-payments by your client.

Bill Clients Regularly

You can manage your cash flows better if you receive regular payments from your clients. Monthly payments are common for consultants who bill expenses and hours. But, you can request clients to pay you every two weeks or every week.

Invoice Immediately

You must send invoices to your clients immediately so that they can pay you sooner.

Use Email

Sending your invoices through snail mail can take many days to arrive. But, if you send them through email, you cut the delivery time of invoices to seconds.

Offer Discounts

To encourage your clients to make prompt payments, you can offer a small discount if they pay early. You may lose a small amount of money. But, prompt payments can ensure that you pay *your* bills on time.

Track Payments

Keep your eye on open invoices and ensure that you follow up payments from your clients. You can call them personally to find out why they miss payments. If clients do not pay you, do not hesitate to start your collection procedures.

Filing Consultant Taxes

If you are a self-employed consultant, you need to follow the rules on paying taxes. You need to shoulder the full amount of Social Security and Medicare. As of 2012, your Social Security payments amount to 10.4% of your total earnings. Your Medicare payments amount to 2.9%. Also, you follow your tax bracket when paying income taxes.

Because you are not an employee, you need to make quarterly tax filings. You need to do so if you believe you need to pay at least $1,000 in taxes for the taxable year. You can deduct your business expenses from your total tax liability.

These expenses can include costs incurred for your home office or external office. However, business travel expenses do not include travel from your home to your work site. In general, you can include expenses necessary to do your job in your tax deductions.

In the USA, you need Form 1040-ES for your quarterly tax filings. If your clients paid you at least $600, they need to use a 1099-MISC. They must also state the amount paid for your services. But, non-receipt of the forms does not mean that you do not pay your taxes. If you are an employee and also work as a freelance consultant, you need to file Form 1040 at year end. If you earn at least $400 a year from your consultancy work, you need to include Schedule C with your Form 1040.

CHAPTER 13: BUILDING AND MAINTAINING WORKING RELATIONSHIPS

If you have just established your consultancy business, you need to market your services, and realize that this job is harder than you think. Your potential clients may not even be aware that they need you.

DIRECT MAIL

You can create interest in your new consultancy business through direct mail. This is an effective marketing strategy because you can reach your targeted audience easily. First, you must create a list of your prospective clients. Then, you send them your brochure, sales letter, or flyer that describes your services.

To be effective, write a personal sales letter and address the recipient by name. You can write a compelling message outside of the envelope. You can use "Act now," "Limited Time Offer," and "Free" to get the attention of the recipient. In your sales letter, draw attention to the benefits of your offer. Include your contact details so that clients can contact you as soon as possible.

COLD CALLS

In cold calling, you contact your prospective clients to sell them your consulting service. Many people do not want to accept cold calls. Although you can have cold calling as one of your marketing strategies, it may not be as effective.

When you make cold calls, you must prepare for rejection. You may need to make at least 30 calls before you can get a client to say yes. Before you make your sales pitch, practice it. You can ask a friend to act as a prospective client. You can ask him for feedback about your sincerity and effectiveness. Then, make the adjustments.

ADVERTISING

You can advertise in specialized magazines or trade journals to save on advertising expense. You can also list your services in specialty sections like a consultants' directory.

NEWSLETTERS

You can send newsletters to clients to inform them of your consulting business. A newsletter can include important news about the industry, editorials, and opinions about consultancy. It can also include tips for success.

REFERRALS

If you have finished your consulting project with a client, you can ask for the referral. You can write a short letter or note thanking him. Then, you use the opportunity to ask for names of people who may need your services.

Companies hire consultants because consultants help them make improvements in their performance. Consultants analyze organizational problems in order to suggest solutions. They offer objective and external advice. They also provide specialized skills that may not be present within the organization. Because of their exposure to different organizational issues, they are in the best position to recommend the best practices to any company. However, not all of these practices are fit for all organizations.

Consultants can take any of these two approaches: prescriptive or facilitative. The prescriptive approach allows them to provide expert advice to clients. However, it requires less input from clients. The facilitative approach allows them to include all other stakeholders in the consultation process.

As a consultant, you provide expert advice in public relations, marketing, education, science, human resources, management, accountancy, finance, security, law, engineering, and other fields. You can provide your service in an area where you have professional experience and deep knowledge. You can be an internal or external consultant. As an internal consultant, you are an employee of a company. You advise different departments or employees about your areas of expertise. As an external consultant, you work for a fee in an organization on a temporary basis.

Although there are no preset qualifications to becoming a consultant, you should have at least a college degree related to your expertise. You may need a professional license in some fields like medicine, psychology, legal, and engineering before you can become a consultant. However, organizations may prefer experience if you have a lengthy, distinguished career.

In addition, you may need to become a member of some consulting organizations. As an accredited consultant, you need to abide by the consulting organization's Code of Ethics. You establish your credibility when you become an accredited consultant. You can become a strategy consultant, management consultant, operations consultant, financial advisory consultant, human resource consultant, or IT consultant.

The consulting business as a result of the recession in 2008 - 2009. In the USA, the Census Bureau estimated the consulting industry to be worth $607 billion in 2015. This amount can grow higher because of globalization. Consulting firms have expanded to other countries like Brazil, China, Europe, India, and North America.

If you are a management consultant, you provide advice to companies in areas that need improvement. You recommend platforms, models, and processes that align with their challenges, strengths, opportunities, and internal and external threats.

To become successful, you can provide your consulting services to a niche. This market segment must be big enough for you to earn money. It is also best that you do not have to deal with many competitors in this niche. You can charge higher per hour if you have specialized skills to offer to your clients.

The first thing that you can do to find a niche is to assess your skills and experience. You need to decide which of your many skills is the most marketable. Then, check if there is demand for these skills. You must find out how much money consultants, who have the same skills like yours, earn. Then, choose your specialty. Perform market research in your chosen specialty to see if you can make a living being a consultant in your chosen niche.

Before you can put up a consulting business, you need to register it first. You must ensure that you have the necessary permits and licenses to operate the business. If your consultancy is home-based and in the USA, you must get a Home Occupation Permit. Also, you need to seek clearance with your homeowner's association if you plan to have a home office.

You also need to prepare your accounting procedures before you can practice your consultancy career.

First, you have to decide on the business structure of your business. You can register an LLC, corporation, or sole proprietorship.

Second, you need to get a Tax Identification Number.

Third, you have to prepare your accounting procedures. You may decide to use accounting software for maintaining your records.

Fourth, you need to open a separate business bank account for your consultancy business.

Fifth, your city may require you to get business insurance. It may need you to get, at least, a professional liability insurance.

Sixth, you need to get licenses and permits.

Seventh, you need to select your business partners.

When you become a consultant, you have to hone your presentation skills. You need to learn PowerPoint because you will use it in your presentations, detailed analysis, and final reports. You have to remember that your presentation must include a precise structure. As such, you need to make your presentations short, concise, and to the point.

You need to send a proposal after you, and your client have reached an agreement. In your proposal, focus on your client and your agreement. Because the proposal supports the process of decision making, you must ensure that its structure is logical. The proposal should be short, simple, clear, and focused on the return-on-investment and output.

In terms of consulting fees, you can use any of the following models: double or triple the hourly wage, daily rate, project-based rate, performance-based rate, actual data rate, solution-based rate, and the prevailing rate charged by other consultants.

It is important to hone your negotiating skills. Aside from the consulting fee, you need to negotiate the travel budget, content rights, high-end coaching, and products and servicing licensing. Before meeting the client, you should already know what you want. You must understand your client's requirements so that you know what expertise and skills to offer him.

When negotiating with a client, take a firm yet polite position. Compromise and focus on the big picture. If you work with a team, you must not commit without first consulting them. The client may request changes to each item in the proposal. You may consider giving in to his demand. These nuances can improve your performance.

If you are negotiating with a client, remember that you can ask for time to think before you agree with him. You must serve your client's needs when you negotiate. Know when to say no. If the negotiation fails, analyze why it fails and what you can do to improve your negotiation skills.

Your new client should receive a welcome kit to familiarize himself with how you conduct your consulting business. The welcome kit includes your short biography, office hours, communication policies, an overview of work processes and operations, instructions for work requests submission, an overview of services, expectations, and frequently-asked-questions.

If you bill your clients, you can ask for advance payments to mitigate the risks of nonpayment or late payments. So that you can manage your cash flows, bill your clients regularly. As soon as you create an invoice, you can send it through email so that your client can receive it immediately.

You can offer discounts for prompt payments. You can monitor payments so that you can follow up with your clients. As a self-employed consultant, you must pay your taxes, Social Security, and Medicare. You need to file quarterly taxes if you think you will pay a minimum of $1,000 taxes for the year.

APPENDIX A: SAMPLE SALES CONSULTING PROPOSAL TEMPLATE

Development of a Formal Sales Process

A formal sales process allows you to systematically manage business opportunities. {my_company} develops this process for you based on a quantitative analysis of your costs, competitors, and customer profile. This customized solution keeps your pipeline of prospects full and ensures your sales force uses its limited resources for the most profitable effect.

Analysis of Current Sales Strategies and Advice to Improve Them

{my_company} will visit {client_name}'s business personally and observe the current sales process there from start to finish. Then, relying on those firsthand observations and an outside perspective, {my_company} will analyze any inefficiencies and offer actionable advice about how to fix them.

Sales Force Training and Counsel

{my_company} will determine how to structure your sales force, its ideal size, and where to assign talent to generate the most profits. We will also use our expertise to train your sales force for maximum efficiency. To ensure that our services meet {client_name}'s needs, {my_company} includes benchmarking and measurement in every contract.

Your Investment

Service Item	Cost

Increasing Sales Performance and Long-term Profitability Solution
 	
    Discovery and sales process analysis – We'll take a look at how much money you're spending, what your competitors are up to, and your target customer profile to figure out what's working well and which areas have the potential for improvement.
 	
    Development of a formal sales process – Using what we learn in our analysis, we'll create a customized system for your sales team to implement that generates consistent leads, turns prospects into buyers, and one-time customers into long-term business partners.
 	
    Sales force training and counsel – We'll meet with your sales executives to deliver our recommendations to improve sales force efficiency. We'll also meet with all the members of your sales team and brief them on how to implement our sales process in the best way.
	$

Total	$

Why Choose {my_company}?

{client_name} wants to excel in every aspect of its business, but it can't afford to lose momentum by only focusing on sales without facing pressure from its competitors. That's why you want a company like {my_company} to provide you with a solution to maximize your sales without compromising your time and strengths. Our expertise, resources, and deep commitment to our craft make us the ideal choice to meet {client_name}'s needs for a sales solution. We'll bring the following strengths to our work for {client_name}:

* {my_company} only hires experienced salespeople – Everyone on our team brings real-world experience to the table. We're doers, not theorists. This wealth of knowledge offers us a unique perspective into the strategies that work and those that don't; we want to share the most effective ones with you.

* {my_company} has expertise in a wide range of industries – Our team has worked with clients in industries ranging from software and professional services to defense contracting and biotech. We've distilled what works, and we can provide an invaluable perspective regardless of your current stage of business development.

* {my_company} focuses on helping you strengthen relationships with customers old and new – We understand running a successful business is all about relationships. Certain "key accounts," comprising roughly 20% of your customers, generate 80% of your sales. We'll help you maintain relations with those key accounts and expand them long into the future. But we don't neglect the crucial importance of leaving new prospects with a good impression, so our sales strategies cover all the bases.

Project Timeline

Should {client_name} choose {my_company} to execute this solution as proposed, our timeline for this project is as follows:

Phase	Activities	Completion
Discovery	Analysis of {client_name}'s costs, competition, customer profile and sales process.	07/31/XX
Sales Process Development	Comprehensive strategy development to guide every aspect of the selling process, from lead-generation to follow-ups and managing existing customers.	08/21/XX
Sales Force Training and Management	Consultations with senior executives and the sales team in which {my_company} will share its findings with the attendees, offer actionable advice, and field any questions.	09/05/XX

Next Steps

As outlined in the Investment section, our pricing is valid until [DATE]. To take advantage of this proposal and proceed with the project as outlined, {client_name}'s next steps must be to:

- Accept the proposal as-is
- Discuss desired changes with {my_company}
- Finalize and sign the contract
- Submit an initial payment of 50 percent of total project fee

Once completed, {my_company} will contact {client_name} to schedule a project launch meeting to make introductions and gather information before beginning the work.

We're happy to make changes to project scope on {client_name}'s request at any time, but may be subject to additional billing.

Terms and Conditions

Once the project fee is paid in full to {my_company}, any elements of text, graphics, photos, contents, trademarks, or other artwork furnished to {client_name} for inclusion in website are owned by {client_name}.

{my_company} assumes {client_name} has permission from the rightful owner to use any code, scripts, data, and reports are provided by {client_name} for inclusion in its materials, and will hold harmless, protect, and defend {my_company} from any claim or suit arising from the use of such work.

{my_company} retains the right to display graphics and other web content elements as examples of their work in their portfolio and as content features in other projects.

This agreement becomes effective only when signed by agents of {client_name} and {my_company}. Regardless of the place of signing of this agreement, {client_name} agrees that for purposes of venue, this contract was entered into in [STATE] and any dispute will be litigated or arbitrated in [STATE].

The agreement contained in this contract constitutes the sole agreement between {client_name} and the {my_company} regarding all items included in this agreement.

Source: http://www.doctemplates.net/consulting-proposal-templates/

APPENDIX B: SAMPLE SIMPLE PROPOSAL TEMPLATE

Monica,

Hello. This is James Richards. As per our last discussion, I am putting a formal consultation plan in writing for your company's review and (hopeful) acceptance in helping design your call center.

I am a twenty-year call center veteran with experience and success in every imaginable facet of the field—from working the phones to running the centers to designing them. Those centers I've redesigned saw near-immediate increases in productivity and revenue, and of the 30 or so I've helped build, only two didn't report a profit the last fiscal year.

The process we discussed would begin with a review of your existing plan, which should take no longer than two days. Sometime after that, we would meet to discuss the results and my proposed changes. This process is a back-and-forth and generally takes two revisions to complete, though my contract allows for five (and is flexible regarding more when needed). Finally, I will help you build the correct team for your center by watching several interviews, coaching you on your style, and reviewing the rest of your candidates.

My design input and knowledge will give you everything you need to get a leg up in the telemarketing world. With me at your side, those bizarre situations and technical issues that seem to have no solution become quick fixes. Whatever your prior experience, my help will make you wise beyond your professional years.

Your company would be responsible for all travel charges incurred and would be required to pay my standard $65 dollar per diem for meals and other day-to-day activities. All other charges are outlined in my contract, but the total would come to roughly $1,363 dollars with the services outlined in this program. Though I am here to be an all-in-one resource, I want to make clear that while I can help with certain technical issues, those that go above my head will need to be handled by IT professionals.

I believe I've offered a fair deal and absolutely amazing value with this proposal; however, if you don't agree with anything you see, please let me know.

Sincerely,

Dave Murphy

Source: http://www.doctemplates.net/consulting-proposal-templates/

APPENDIX C: IRS APPLICATION FOR EMPLOYER IDENTIFICATION NUMBER

https://www.irs.gov/businesses/small-businesses-self-employed/how-to-apply-for-an-ein

---

Form SS-4
(Rev. January 2010)
Department of the Treasury
Internal Revenue Service

Application for Employer Identification Number

(For use by employers, corporations, partnerships, trusts, estates, churches, government agencies, Indian tribal entities, certain individuals, and others.)
► See separate instructions for each line. ► Keep a copy for your records.

OMB No. 1545-0003
EIN

Type or print clearly.

1. Legal name of entity (or individual) for whom the EIN is being requested

2. Trade name of business (if different from name on line 1)

3. Executor, administrator, trustee, "care of" name

4a. Mailing address (room, apt., suite no. and street, or P.O. box)
5a. Street address (if different) (Do not enter a P.O. box.)

4b. City, state, and ZIP code (if foreign, see instructions)
5b. City, state, and ZIP code (if foreign, see instructions)

6. County and state where principal business is located

7a. Name of responsible party
7b. SSN, ITIN, or EIN

8a. Is this application for a limited liability company (LLC) (or a foreign equivalent)? ☐ Yes ☐ No
8b. If 8a is "Yes," enter the number of LLC members . . . . . ►

8c. If 8a is "Yes," was the LLC organized in the United States? . . . . ☐ Yes ☐ No

9a. Type of entity (check only one box). Caution. If 8a is "Yes," see the instructions for the correct box to check.
☐ Sole proprietor (SSN)
☐ Partnership
☐ Corporation (enter form number to be filed) ►
☐ Personal service corporation
☐ Church or church-controlled organization
☐ Other nonprofit organization (specify) ►
☐ Other (specify) ►
☐ Estate (SSN of decedent)
☐ Plan administrator (TIN)
☐ Trust (TIN of grantor)
☐ National Guard ☐ State/local government
☐ Farmers' cooperative ☐ Federal government/military
☐ REMIC ☐ Indian tribal governments/enterprises
Group Exemption Number (GEN) if any ►

9b. If a corporation, name the state or foreign country (if applicable) where incorporated
State | Foreign country

10. Reason for applying (check only one box)
☐ Started new business (specify type) ►
☐ Hired employees (Check the box and see line 13.)
☐ Compliance with IRS withholding regulations
☐ Other (specify) ►
☐ Banking purpose (specify purpose) ►
☐ Changed type of organization (specify new type) ►
☐ Purchased going business
☐ Created a trust (specify type) ►
☐ Created a pension plan (specify type) ►

11. Date business started or acquired (month, day, year). See instructions.
12. Closing month of accounting year

13. Highest number of employees expected in the next 12 months (enter -0- if none). If no employees expected, skip line 14.

Agricultural	Household	Other

14. If you expect your employment tax liability to be $1,000 or less in a full calendar year and want to file Form 944 annually instead of Forms 941 quarterly, check here. (Your employment tax liability generally will be $1,000 or less if you expect to pay $4,000 or less in total wages.) If you do not check this box, you must file Form 941 for every quarter. ☐

15. First date wages or annuities were paid (month, day, year). Note. If applicant is a withholding agent, enter date income will first be paid to nonresident alien (month, day, year) . . . . ►

16. Check one box that best describes the principal activity of your business. ☐ Health care & social assistance ☐ Wholesale-agent/broker
☐ Construction ☐ Rental & leasing ☐ Transportation & warehousing ☐ Accommodation & food service ☐ Wholesale-other ☐ Retail
☐ Real estate ☐ Manufacturing ☐ Finance & insurance ☐ Other (specify) ►

17. Indicate principal line of merchandise sold, specific construction work done, products produced, or services provided.

18. Has the applicant entity shown on line 1 ever applied for and received an EIN? ☐ Yes ☐ No
If "Yes," write previous EIN here ►

Third Party Designee
Complete this section only if you want to authorize the named individual to receive the entity's EIN and answer questions about the completion of this form.
Designee's name | Designee's telephone number (include area code)
Address and ZIP code | Designee's fax number (include area code)

Under penalties of perjury, I declare that I have examined this application, and to the best of my knowledge and belief, it is true, correct, and complete.
Applicant's telephone number (include area code)
Name and title (type or print clearly) ►
Applicant's fax number (include area code)

STATE OF ALABAMA:

COUNTY OF MADISON:

ARTICLES OF ORGANIZATION

OF

HUDSON CONSULTING GROUP LLC

The undersigned, acting as organizers of the Hudson Consulting Group LLC under the Alabama Limited Liability Company Act, adopt the following Articles of Organization for said Limited Liability Company.

Article I

Name of the Company

The name of the limited liability company is Hudson Consulting Group LLC (the "Company").

Article II

Period of Duration

The period of duration is ninety (90) years from the date of filing of these Articles of Organization with the Alabama Secretary of State, unless the Company is sooner dissolved.

Article III

Purpose of the Company

The Company is organized to engage in all legal and lawful purpose of Business Consulting business.

Article IV

Registered Office and Agent

The Company's registered office is at address is 123 Main Court, Huntsville, Alabama 35801; and the name and the address of the Company's initial registered agent is John Doe, 123 Main Court, Huntsville, Alabama 35801.

.

Article V

Members of the Organization

There are two (2) members, all of which are identified in the Exhibit A attached hereto and a part hereof. The initial capital contribution agreed to be made by both members are also listed on Exhibit A. The members have not agreed to make any additional contributions, but may agree to do so in the future upon the terms and conditions as set forth in the Operating Agreement.

Article VI

Additional Members

The members, as identified in the Company's Operating Agreement, reserve the right to admit additional members and determine the Capital Contributions of such Members. Notwithstanding the foregoing, the additional Members may not become managing unless and until selected to such position as provided in Article VII of the Company's Operating Agreement.

Article VII

Contribution upon Withdrawal of Members

The members shall have the right to continue the company upon the death, retirement, resignation, expulsion, bankruptcy or dissolution of a member or occurrence of any event which terminates the continued membership of a member in the Company (collectively, "Withdrawal"), as long as there is at least One remaining member, and the remaining member agree to continue the Company by unanimous written consent within 90 days after the Withdrawal of a Member, as set forth in the Operating Agreement of the Company.

Article VIII

Manager

The name and business address of the initial manager is:

John Doe

Hudson Consulting Group LLC

123 Main Court

Huntsville, Alabama 35801

The manager may be removed and replaced by the Members as provided in the Operating Agreement.

IN WITNESS WHEREOF, the undersigned have caused these Articles of Organization to be executed this …………… Day of ……………………… 2016

_____

_____

Hudson Consulting Group LLC

DATE

AN ALABAMA CORPORATION

BY: John Doe

ITS: Managing Member

This instrument prepared by:

Jane Doe

999 Super Ct

Huntsville, Alabama 35801

EXHIBIT A

MEMBERS	INTIAL CONTRIBUTION	INTEREST
John Doe	Future Services Rendered	50%
Jane Doe	Future Services Rendered	50%

APPENDIX E: SAMPLE CONSULTING AGREEMENT

HUDSON CONSULTING GROUP

CONSULTING AGREEMENT

This Consulting Agreement (this "Agreement") is made as of _____, by and between [Company Name], a Delaware corporation (the "Company"), and _____ ("Consultant").

Consulting Relationship. During the term of this Agreement, Consultant will provide consulting services to the Company as described on Exhibit A hereto (the "Services"). Consultant represents that Consultant is duly licensed (as applicable) and has the qualifications, the experience and the ability to properly perform the Services. Consultant shall use Consultant's best efforts to perform the Services such that the results are satisfactory to the Company. Consultant shall devote [at least] [_____% of Consultant's time/_____ hours per week] to performance of the Services.

Fees. As consideration for the Services to be provided by Consultant and other obligations, the Company shall pay to Consultant the amounts specified in Exhibit B hereto at the times specified therein.

Expenses. Consultant shall not be authorized to incur on behalf of the Company any expenses and will be responsible for all expenses incurred while performing the Services [except as expressly specified in Exhibit C hereto] unless otherwise agreed to by the Company's [Title of Officer], which consent shall be evidenced in writing for any expenses in excess of $_____. As a condition to receipt of reimbursement, Consultant shall be required to submit to the Company reasonable evidence that the amount involved was both reasonable and necessary to the Services provided under this Agreement.

Term and Termination. Consultant shall serve as a consultant to the Company for a period commencing on _____ and terminating on the earlier of (a) the date Consultant completes the provision of the Services to the Company under this Agreement, or (b) the date Consultant shall have been paid the maximum amount of consulting fees as provided in Exhibit B hereto.

Notwithstanding the above, either party may terminate this Agreement at any time upon _____ business days' written notice. In the event of such termination, Consultant shall be paid for any portion of the Services that have been performed prior to the termination.

Should either party default in the performance of this Agreement or materially breach any of its obligations under this Agreement, including but not limited to Consultant's obligations under the Confidential Information and Invention Assignment Agreement between the Company and Consultant referenced below, the non-breaching party may terminate this Agreement immediately if the breaching party fails to cure the breach within _____ business days after having received written notice by the non-breaching party of the breach or default.

Independent Contractor. Consultant's relationship with the Company will be that of an independent contractor and not that of an employee.

Method of Provision of Services. Consultant shall be solely responsible for determining the method, details and means of performing the Services. Consultant may, at Consultant's own expense, employ or engage the services of such employees, subcontractors, partners or agents, as Consultant deems necessary to perform the Services (collectively, the "Assistants"). The Assistants are not and shall not be employees of the Company, and Consultant shall be wholly responsible for the professional performance of the Services by the Assistants such that the results are satisfactory to the Company. Consultant shall expressly advise the Assistants of the terms of this Agreement, and shall require each Assistant to execute and deliver to the Company a Confidential Information and Invention Assignment Agreement substantially in the form attached to this Agreement as Exhibit D hereto (the "Confidentiality Agreement").

No Authority to Bind Company. Consultant acknowledges and agrees that Consultant and its Assistants have no authority to enter into contracts that bind the Company or create obligations on the part of the Company without the prior written authorization of the Company.

No Benefits. Consultant acknowledges and agrees that Consultant and its Assistants shall not be eligible for any Company employee benefits and, to the extent Consultant otherwise would be eligible for any Company employee benefits but for the express terms of this Agreement, Consultant (on behalf of itself and its employees) hereby expressly declines to participate in such Company employee benefits.

Withholding; Indemnification. Consultant shall have full responsibility for applicable withholding taxes for all compensation paid to Consultant or its Assistants under this Agreement, and for compliance with all applicable labor and employment requirements with respect to Consultant's self-employment, sole proprietorship or other form of business organization, and with respect to the Assistants, including state worker's compensation insurance coverage requirements and any U.S. immigration visa requirements. Consultant agrees to indemnify, defend and hold the Company harmless from any liability for, or assessment of, any claims or penalties with respect to such withholding taxes, labor or employment requirements, including any liability for, or assessment of, withholding taxes imposed on the Company by the relevant taxing authorities with respect to any compensation paid to Consultant or its Assistants.

Supervision of Consultant's Services. All of the services to be performed by Consultant, including but not limited to the Services, will be as agreed between Consultant and the Company's [Supervisor's Title]. Consultant will be required to report to the [Supervisor's Title] concerning the Services performed under this Agreement. The nature and frequency of these reports will be left to the discretion of the [Supervisor's Title].

Consulting or Other Services for Competitors. Consultant represents and warrants that Consultant does not presently perform or intend to perform, during the term of the Agreement, consulting or other services for, or engage in or intend to engage in an employment relationship with, companies whose businesses or proposed businesses in any way involve products or services which would be competitive with the Company's products or services, or those products or services proposed or in development by the Company during the term of the Agreement (except for those companies, if any, listed on Exhibit E hereto). If, however, Consultant decides to do so, Consultant agrees that, in advance of accepting such work, Consultant will promptly notify the Company in writing, specifying the organization with which Consultant proposes to consult, provide services, or become employed by and to provide information sufficient to allow the Company to determine if such work would conflict with the terms of this Agreement, including the terms of the Confidentiality Agreement, the interests of the Company or further services which the Company might request of Consultant. If the Company determines that such work conflicts with the terms of this Agreement, the Company reserves the right to terminate this Agreement immediately. In no event shall any of the Services be performed for the Company at the facilities of a third party or using the resources of a third party.

Confidential Information and Invention Assignment Agreement. Consultant shall sign, or has signed, a Confidential Information and Invention Assignment Agreement in the form set forth as Exhibit D hereto, on or before the date Consultant begins providing the Services.

Conflicts with this Agreement. Consultant represents and warrants that neither Consultant nor any of the Assistants is under any pre-existing obligation in conflict or in any way inconsistent with the provisions of this Agreement. Consultant represents and warrants that Consultant's performance of all the terms of this Agreement will not breach any agreement to keep in confidence proprietary information acquired by Consultant in confidence or in trust prior to commencement of this Agreement. Consultant warrants that Consultant has the right to disclose and/or or use all ideas, processes, techniques and other information, if any, which Consultant has gained from third parties, and which Consultant discloses to the Company or uses in the course of performance of this Agreement, without liability to such third parties. Notwithstanding the foregoing, Consultant agrees that Consultant shall not bundle with or incorporate into any deliveries provided to the Company herewith any third party products, ideas, processes, or other techniques, without the express, written prior approval of the Company. Consultant represents and warrants that Consultant has not granted and will not grant any rights or licenses to any intellectual property or technology that would conflict with Consultant's obligations under this Agreement. Consultant will not knowingly infringe upon any copyright, patent, trade secret or other property right of any former client, employer or third party in the performance of the Services.

Miscellaneous.

Governing Law. The validity, interpretation, construction and performance of this Agreement, and all acts and transactions pursuant hereto and the rights and obligations of the parties hereto shall be governed, construed and interpreted in accordance with the laws of the state of California, without giving effect to principles of conflicts of law.

Entire Agreement. This Agreement sets forth the entire agreement and understanding of the parties relating to the subject matter herein and supersedes all prior or contemporaneous discussions, understandings and agreements, whether oral or written, between them relating to the subject matter hereof.

Amendments and Waivers. No modification of or amendment to this Agreement, nor any waiver of any rights under this Agreement, shall be effective unless in writing signed by the parties to this Agreement. No delay or failure to require performance of any provision of this Agreement shall constitute a waiver of that provision as to that or any other instance.

Successors and Assigns. Except as otherwise provided in this Agreement, this Agreement, and the rights and obligations of the parties hereunder, will be binding upon and inure to the benefit of their respective successors, assigns, heirs, executors, administrators and legal representatives. The Company may assign any of its rights and obligations under this Agreement. No other party to this Agreement may assign, whether voluntarily or by operation of law, any of its rights and obligations under this Agreement, except with the prior written consent of the Company.

Notices. Any notice, demand or request required or permitted to be given under this Agreement shall be in writing and shall be deemed sufficient when delivered personally or by overnight courier or sent by email, or 48 hours after being deposited in the U.S. mail as certified or registered mail with postage prepaid, addressed to the party to be notified at such party's address as set forth on the signature page, as subsequently modified by written notice, or if no address is specified on the signature page, at the most recent address set forth in the Company's books and records.

Severability. If one or more provisions of this Agreement are held to be unenforceable under applicable law, the parties agree to renegotiate such provision in good faith. In the event that the parties cannot reach a mutually agreeable and enforceable replacement for such provision, then (i) such provision shall be excluded from this Agreement, (ii) the balance of the Agreement shall be interpreted as if such provision were so excluded and (iii) the balance of the Agreement shall be enforceable in accordance with its terms.

Construction. This Agreement is the result of negotiations between and has been reviewed by each of the parties hereto and their respective counsel, if any; accordingly, this Agreement shall be deemed to be the product of all of the parties hereto, and no ambiguity shall be construed in favor of or against any one of the parties hereto.

Counterparts. This Agreement may be executed in any number of counterparts, each of which when so executed and delivered shall be deemed an original, and all of which together shall constitute one and the same agreement. Execution of a facsimile copy will have the same force and effect as execution of an original, and a facsimile signature will be deemed an original and valid signature.

Electronic Delivery. The Company may, in its sole discretion, decide to deliver any documents related to this Agreement or any notices required by applicable law or the Company's Certificate of Incorporation or Bylaws by email or any other electronic means. Consultant hereby consents to (i) conduct business electronically (ii) receive such documents and notices by such electronic delivery and (iii) sign documents electronically and agrees to participate through an on-line or electronic system established and maintained by the Company or a third party designated by the Company.

The parties have executed this Agreement as of the date first written above.

THE COMPANY:

HUDSON CONSULTING GROUP

By:

(Signature)

Name:
Title:

Address:

_____

_____ _____
United States

CONSULTANT:

(PRINT NAME)

(Signature)

Address

Email:

EXHIBIT A

DESCRIPTION OF CONSULTING SERVICES

<u>Description of Services</u>   <u>Schedule/Deadline</u>

1.

2.

EXHIBIT B

COMPENSATION

Check applicable payment terms:

[ ]   For Services rendered by Consultant under this Agreement, the Company shall pay Consultant at the rate of $____ per hour, payable _____. Unless otherwise agreed upon in writing by Company, Company's maximum liability for all Services performed during the term of this Agreement shall not exceed $_____.

[ ]   Consultant shall be paid $_____ upon the execution of this Agreement and $_____ upon completion of the Services specified on Exhibit A to this Agreement.

[ ]   The Company will recommend that the Board grant a non-qualified option to purchase _____ shares of the Company's Common Stock, at an exercise price equal to the fair market value (as determined by the Company's Board of Directors) on the date of grant, and which will vest and become exercisable as follows:

[ ]   Other:

EXHIBIT C

ALLOWABLE EXPENSES

EXHIBIT D

CONFIDENTIAL INFORMATION AND INVENTION ASSIGNMENT AGREEMENT

[See Attached]

EXHIBIT E

LIST OF COMPANIES
EXCLUDED UNDER SECTION 8

___ No conflicts

___ Additional Sheets Attached

Signature of Consultant: _____

Print Name of Consultant: _____

Date: _____

Made in the USA
Middletown, DE
23 December 2017